KU-210-877

Bare necessities

Poverty and Social Exclusion in Northern Ireland

Bare necessities

Poverty and Social Exclusion in Northern Ireland:

key findings

Paddy Hillyard, Grace Kelly, Eithne McLaughlin, Demi Patsios and Mike Tomlinson

democratic
dialogue

Democratic Dialogue
report 16
October 2003

Democratic Dialogue
23 University Street
Belfast BT7 1FY
Tel: +44-(0)28-9022-0050
Fax: +44-(0)28-9022-0051
e-mail: info@democraticdialogue.org
Web site: http://www.democraticdialogue.org

© Democratic Dialogue 2003
ISBN 1 900281 15 5

Cover design by Dunbar Design
Cover photograph: Oistín Mac Bride

Printed by Colour Books Ltd, Dublin

Contents

Preface

This is the 16th report from the think tank Democratic Dialogue. DD gratefully acknowledges the financial assistance for this project from the Office of the First Minister and Deputy First Minister in Northern Ireland. DD also greatly values the core funding it currently receives from the Community Relations Council, the Esmee Fairbairn Foundation and Queen's University Belfast.

Comments on the publication are very welcome. Anyone wishing to be kept informed of DD projects and events should e-mail the organisation via info@democraticdialogue.org; e-mailings are sent out every month or so.

Further copies of this report are available from DD, price £7.50 (£10 institutions, £4.00 unwaged) plus 10 per cent postage and packing. Our catalogue of publications is available, along with more information about DD and other projects, on our web site: http://www.democraticdialogue.org

Acknowledgements

The research on which this report is based was funded by the Office of the First Minister and Deputy First Minister, the Department of Finance and Personnel, and with support from the Treasury's evidence-based policy fund.

We have benefited from the expertise and guidance of many people during the course of the research. In the early stages we had fruitful discussions with members of the project steering group: Frances Dowds (Northern Ireland Anti-Poverty Network), Graeme Hutchinson (Department of Finance and Personnel), Stephanie Harcourt (Department of Health, Social Services and Public Safety), Alan McClelland (Office of the First Minister and Deputy First Minister), Andrew McCormick (Central Survey Unit, Northern Ireland Statistics and Research Agency), Kevin Sweeney (Central Survey Unit, Northern Ireland Statistics and Research Agency) and Margaret Ward (Democratic Dialogue). Our thanks to the research staff who have been involved in the project: Maria Bergstrom and Caroline McAuley.

During the survey stages, Suzanne Bradley, Peter Scott and Andrew McCormick (Central Survey Unit) were especially helpful. Alan McClelland (OFM/DFM) has been particularly attentive throughout the project, always responding quickly and with sound advice at critical points. Special advisors to the project, Dorothy Watson (Economic and Social Research Institute, Dublin) Dave Gordon (Director, The Townsend Centre for International Poverty Research, Bristol University), Kevin Balanda (Institute of Public Health, Dublin and Belfast) and Roger O'Sullivan (Rural Community Network) provided essential advice on the construction of poverty measures, equivalisation, comparative methodologies and health indicators.

We are especially grateful to Dave Gordon for detailed guidance and support – at all times of the day and night – on the construction of consensual poverty.

Without the initial support and ongoing enthusiasm for the research from Stephen Donnelly (OFM/DFM), it is probable that Northern Ireland would still be lacking a publicly available, benchmark statement of poverty levels.

Finally, our thanks go to all the CSU survey field force and the 3,104 people who responded to the survey.

All of the above have contributed in some way to this report, but we alone take responsibility for its contents.

Paddy Hillyard (University of Ulster)
Grace Kelly (Queen's University)
Eithne McLaughlin (Queen's University)
Demi Patsios (University of Bristol)
Mike Tomlinson (Queen's University)

August 2003

Chapter 1
Introduction

For many years, Northern Ireland was recognised to be one of the most deprived parts of the United Kingdom. It has not featured strongly in debates over either the measurement of poverty, or poverty alleviation policies. In particular, Northern Ireland has no tradition of publishing household income data which would allow comparisons with other regions and countries.

This study begins to redress these gaps and to provide a benchmark for poverty measurement in Northern Ireland in the future. The research should inform debates on the future direction of poverty reduction policies.

The core aims of the research were:

1. to provide a baseline, early 21st century measurement of poverty and social exclusion which can be updated periodically in the future.

2. to provide data on the extent to which poverty and social exclusion vary across the nine dimensions of equality specified in Section 75 of the Northern Ireland Act 1998; and

3. to compare poverty levels in Northern Ireland with results of research on low incomes, poverty and social exclusion in Britain and poverty levels in the Republic of Ireland.

Two surveys were carried out between June 2002 and January 2003. In the first survey, a random sample of people were asked to say which material items and social activities they regarded as necessities of life at the start of the 21st century. The responses were used to establish a social consensus on the items and activities people in Northern Ireland think everybody should be able to afford and should not have to do without. The second survey identified the numbers of households lacking particular necessities.

The survey evidence on deprivation was then combined with household income to establish a measure of poverty. The extent to which this approach differs from poverty and social exclusion measures elsewhere is the main focus of Chapter 2. The chapter also discusses international obligations regarding poverty definition and measurement, as well as developments at European Union level designed to replace the simple – and arguably 'meaningless' (Gordon *et al*, 2000b: 93) – measures of low incomes.

Chapter 3 discusses in detail the research design and the method used to calculate the poverty threshold for Northern Ireland. The scope of both surveys is described and while these replicated research carried out in Britain, a different poverty threshold emerged reflecting lower income levels and a higher number of deprivation items.

The report then presents, in Chapter 4, the findings from the two surveys on necessities and the numbers of households and people below the consensual poverty threshold in Northern Ireland. Direct comparisons are made with the equivalent research carried out in Britain.

Chapter 5 compares a number of poverty measures in Britain and the Republic of Ireland with the same measures if they were used in Northern Ireland. This is not a simple exercise because different low income and poverty measures rely on different 'equivalisation' scales for standardising household income. Incomes have to be recalculated for each comparison being made. The chapter begins by describing four different equivalence scales, showing how each of them affects the Northern Ireland household income data. Only then are Northern Ireland statistics on poverty and low income comparable with those published for the Republic of Ireland and Great Britain. Finally, the chapter presents evidence from the surveys about the extent of income inequality in Northern Ireland.

Chapter 6 looks at poverty and social exclusion within Northern Ireland. Poverty rates are presented for each of the dimensions of social equality listed in Section 75 of the 1998 Northern Ireland Act. This chapter also reports on how far people think their own household incomes fall below the poverty threshold.

Finally, Chapter 7 looks at a number of dimensions of social exclusion, giving the survey results for employment, housing, access to services, social participation, personal safety and imprisonment, before the concluding Chapter 8.

Chapter 2
Measuring Poverty and Social Exclusion

Poverty measurement

Over the last decade there have been a number of important developments in poverty measurement as a result of growing concern at international level about widening social and economic inequalities and the persistence of poverty. In 1995 the United Nations (UN) convened a Summit for Social Development at which 117 countries agreed two definitions of poverty, an 'absolute' and 'overall' definition. The Summit also agreed that governments at local, national and regional levels should develop clear plans for the measurement and reduction of overall poverty and the *eradication* of absolute poverty.

In the EU it was agreed in 2000 to adopt a strategy for eradicating poverty and social exclusion. The agreement took the form of four commonly agreed objectives and the preparation of National Action Plans for Social Inclusion (NAPsincl) and periodic

The UN's definition of absolute poverty:

A condition characterised by severe deprivation of basic human needs, including food, safe drinking water, sanitation facilities, health, shelter, education and information. It depends not only on income but also on access to services (UN, 1995:75).

The UN's definition of overall poverty:

[Poverty includes] lack of income and productive resources sufficient to ensure sustainable livelihoods; hunger and malnutrition; ill health; limited or lack of access to education and other basic services; increased morbidity and mortality from illness; homelessness and inadequate housing; unsafe environments; and social discrimination and exclusion. It is also characterized by a lack of participation in decision-making and in civil, social and cultural life. It occurs in all countries: as mass poverty in many developing countries, pockets of poverty amid wealth in developed countries, loss of livelihoods as a result of economic recession, sudden poverty as a result of disaster or conflict, the poverty of low-wage workers, and the utter destitution of people who fall outside family support systems, social institutions and safety nets (UN, 1995: 57).

reporting and monitoring of progress. The latter requires the collection and reporting of comparable statistics on income and social exclusion. This is the purpose of the EU-SILC (Statistics on Income and Living Conditions) data series to be published from 2003 onwards. Eighteen indicators – the so-called 'Laeken indicators' (after the Laeken European Council, December 2001) – are used to monitor poverty and social exclusion. These include monetary indicators and a set of non-monetary indicators covering employ-ment, education and health. The first report was published in April 2003 (Eurostat, 2003).

The Republic of Ireland followed up the UN agreements with a National Anti-Poverty Strategy (Government of Ireland, 1997). The strategy included an official definition of poverty, two measures of poverty – 'consistent' and 'overall' poverty – and targets for their reduction. The United Kingdom (UK) however has not formally adopted a definition of poverty nor, as yet, a measure of poverty for the one social group – children – for which it has adopted a poverty reduction target (Department for Work and Pensions, 2003b).

The Republic of Ireland's National Anti-Poverty Strategy defined and measured consistent poverty as 'equivalised' household income below 50 and 60 per cent of the average

---

Republic of Ireland National Anti-Poverty Strategy

Definition of poverty:

People are living in poverty if their income and resources (material, cultural and social) are so inadequate as to preclude them from having a standard of living which is regarded as acceptable by Irish society generally. As a result of inadequate income and resources people may be excluded and marginalised from participating in activities which are considered the norm for other people in society (Government of Ireland, 1997: 3).

Definition of consistent poverty:

Less than 50 or 60 per cent mean household income plus enforced lack of at least one of eight indicators of 'basic' deprivation.

Definition of overall poverty:

Less than 50 or 60 per cent mean household income.

Definition of equivalisation of income:

A technical process of giving different weights to individuals in a household so that the incomes of different types of households are put on an equivalent basis and may be compared.

---

combined with involuntary lack of at least one of a set of eight expert selected indicators of 'basic' deprivation (Government of Ireland, 1997: 3). Although increasingly questioned as out of date, the eight basic necessities are still regarded as useful for measuring changes in consistent poverty over time (Nolan *et al*, 2002). The UK report *Measuring Child Poverty* however commented that, 'statistical [and expert] approaches to the selection of non-monetary indicators of deprivation are less transparent than asking people their opinion' (Department for Work and Pensions, 2003a: 26). The other Republic of Ireland poverty measure, 'overall poverty', is based on low household income alone.

The UK Government has no definition of poverty. It publishes two sets of poverty related statistics each year. Neither includes Northern Ireland. The first uses household income data drawn from the Family Resources Survey (FRS) and is published annually as The Households Below Average Income Series (HBAI). The HBAI reports the proportions of adults and children below various income thresholds using a number of measures of equivalised household incomes.

In Northern Ireland there has been no income data series comparable to the FRS, although this will change after 2003 as the FRS is now being carried out in Northern Ireland. Income data has been collected in the Continuous Household Survey for many years, but it is only recently that any analysis of income statistics based on this data has been published

(Dignan and McLaughlin, 2002; Dignan, 2003).

Traditionally, HBAI has defined low-income households in terms of thresholds of *mean* income. In November 1998, the European Union agreed that thresholds of *median* income should be used instead. The income threshold used to define the risk of poverty within the EU is now typically 60 per cent of the national median equivalised income per household.

The disadvantage of the HBAI approach is that it provides measures of relative income only. Although relative income is important for understanding the risk of poverty and changes in income inequalities over time, it does not measure the consequences of persistent low incomes in terms of deprivation, low standards of living and social exclusion (Department for Work and Pensions, 2003a).

The UK Government's latest thinking on poverty measurement favours a 'tiered' approach for the future involving income and other measures. It considers that 'a better measure of living standards can be obtained by measuring both low income and material hardship' (Department for Work and Pensions, 2003b: 26).

The second set of UK poverty statistics is published in the annual report *Opportunity For All*, available from 1999 onwards (see for example Department for Work and Pensions, 2001) and reflecting the work of the New Policy Institute (Howarth *et al*, 1999; Rahman *et al*, 2000; Rahman *et al*, 2001; Palmer *et al*, 2002). The reports monitor deprivation on three dimensions: poverty and low income, stage in the family life cycle and 'communities' or localities. Together these dimensions constitute an implicit concept of poverty and social exclusion measured with 50 separate social indicators (Palmer *et al*, 2002) and they go some way to meet the requirements of the UN agreements on poverty. However, because most of the indicators are based on administrative data and are chosen for reasons of availability rather than robustness, they are more a reflection of policy priorities and public service activities than measures of poverty or social exclusion as such.

The multiple indicator approach of *Opportunity For All* is also not a substitute for a single measure of either poverty or social exclusion from which the rise and fall of poverty can be judged. The emphasis attached to results within particular domains, and between domains, is vulnerable to political influence and change over time. Finally, the explanatory power of multiple indicator approaches is limited because it is difficult to draw a cause and effect line between policy, policy impact and indicator change over time.

The Northern Ireland Executive's Programme for Government declared:

> We recognise the inequalities in the life experiences of our citizens in terms of poverty, health, housing, educational and economic opportunity and disability and we are determined to tackle them.
> (2001, para 1.3)

Prior to suspension in 2003 it had not, however, produced an agreed definition or measure of poverty. Considerable effort had been directed to measurement of multiple deprivation on a geographical basis using administrative data. The spatial mapping of multiple deprivation as a substitute for poverty measurement has been characteristic of social policy in Northern Ireland since the 1970s (Noble *et al*, 2001; Tomlinson, 2001; Dignan and McLaughlin, 2002; Tomlinson and Kelly, 2003), and risks missing the target by avoiding the economic and social structural causes of poverty (Quirk and McLaughlin, 1996).

The latest multiple deprivation spatial index is The Northern Ireland Index of Deprivation (Noble *et al*, 2001). This utilises indicators organised into seven domains: low income, employability and unemployment, health and well-being, education, access to services, social environment and housing. In terms of poverty measurement, the index shares the same disadvantages as the *Opportunity For All* multiple indicator approach.

PSE consensual poverty

The British Millennium Poverty and Social Exclusion Survey, funded by the Joseph Rowntree Foundation, was carried out in 1999 by a large team of researchers from Bristol, Loughborough and York Universities (Gordon *et al*, 2000a).

Like the Republic of Ireland consistent poverty measure, the British PSE survey (PSEB) also used a combination of income and deprivation to define poverty but the method differs in that a sample of the general public were asked to decide what the basic necessities of life are. Therefore a poverty consensus is used to define indicators of deprivation.

All definitions and measures of poverty involve some element of political choice. The method of poverty measurement used in PSEB mainly relies on public opinion for these choices. It minimises the expert judgements that have to be made in combining income with other indicators. The authors therefore argue that they have devised a methodology which 'combines a representative popular basis for agreeing what are necessities, with a scientific basis for establishing a level of poverty' (Gordon *et al*, 2000a:

11). For these reasons, it is the method used to produce the headline poverty figures for Northern Ireland given in chapter 4 and for the discussion of equality and poverty in Chapter 6.

Social exclusion

Social exclusion is a concept closely related to poverty. It represents particular challenges to measurement because it has been given such a wide variety of meanings. These range from labour market exclusion (unemployment and 'inactivity'), to exclusion from participation in social life and customs (Levitas, 1998). As a concept, social exclusion takes the focus away from material deprivation and on to other dimensions of social deprivation and exclusion which are not necessarily contingent on income. Above all, many commentators regard social exclusion as a set of 'processes' rather than a material status (Giddens, 1998).

The PSEB and Northern Ireland Poverty and Social Exclusion (PSENI) surveys asked a range of questions designed to explore various dimensions of exclusion, including service exclusion (e.g. lack of telephone, electricity disconnection), exclusion from social relations (various measures of social isolation), and labour market exclusion. Preliminary findings on several dimensions of exclusion are presented in Chapter 7.

Conclusion

Until quite recently, official statistics of poverty relied on measures of relative income alone. The World Summit for Social Development as well as agreements at EU level have stimulated a broader approach which combines relative income measures with non-monetary indicators of deprivation and social exclusion. This provides a more realistic basis for comparing countries but does not necessarily resolve the question of how to differentiate the poor from the non-poor. The PSEB method of combining income and other indicators of deprivation provides a consensual poverty threshold, which is described in detail in the next chapter.

Chapter 3
Research Design and Method

This chapter describes the main method used to measure the nature and extent of poverty and social exclusion in Northern Ireland. With minor refinements, it replicates the consensual mixed income-deprivation approach used in the PSEB.

What are the bare necessities?

The PSEB study developed the 'consensus indicators' approach first used by Mack and Lansley (1985). A representative sample of the population were asked which items and activities they considered to be necessities of life. Then it asked another representative sample which of those items and activities, defined as necessities by more than 50 per cent of respondents, they did not have. If the household did not have the item, they were asked if this was because they did not want it, it was not available or was unsuitable, or they could not afford it. A 'poverty threshold' was then calculated using a range of sequential statistical procedures to relate the number of necessities lacking in a household to the incomes of households. The procedures maximised the differences between the 'poor' and the 'not poor', and minimised the differences within these groups. The resulting poverty threshold for Britain was defined in terms of a household on low income and lacking two or more necessities.

The PSENI research involved the same two stages. Ten of the items and activities used in Britain were not used for a variety of reasons and 19 new items were added to the list of potential necessities. Some minor changes to the wording of other items and activities were also made in the interests of clarity or adaptation in the Northern Ireland context. In total 90 items and activities relevant to both adults and children were used. These included for example a 'warm, waterproof coat', 'visiting friends or family in hospital', 'medicines prescribed by a doctor', 'fresh fruit or vegetables at least once a day', a 'garden to play in', a 'computer suitable for doing homework', a 'dictionary' and 'access to a decent pension'. The full list of items and the proportion of people defining them as necessary is reported in Chapter 4.

n June 2002 a 'Necessities module' was included in the Northern Ireland Statistics and Research Agency's Omnibus Survey, which is conducted on a regular basis by the Central Survey Unit. This survey is based on a random sample of 2,000 addresses drawn from the Valuation and Lands Agency list of

---

PSENI Survey I: The Omnibus Survey Necessities Module

Response Rate 60%

---

addresses. After selecting one household at the assigned address, interviewers listed all the people in the household and the interviewer's computer, then randomly selected one person for interview. One thousand and seventy interviews were successfully achieved from 1,790 addresses, a 60 per cent response rate. Everyone interviewed was shown the list of 90 items and activities and asked which ones they regarded as necessities, that is 'something everyone should be able to afford and should not have to do

without'.

The findings showed broad consensus within Northern Ireland on the necessities of life for both adults and children. There were a few differences between subgroups of the population, but these were not extensive (see McAuley *et al*, 2003). One difference was between the way men and women saw 'personal' and 'household' consumption, with men tending more than women to prioritise items which satisfied personal needs above those which related to household needs. Some significant differences between Northern Ireland and Britain also emerged, particularly in relation to church attendance and a few material items. But perhaps the most significant finding was the extent of consensus across traditional social divides such as religion on what constitutes necessities of life and the minimum standard of living in Northern Ireland (See McAuley *et al*, 2003).

In the second stage of the research a different random sample of 3,490 addresses was drawn from the Valuation and Lands Agency list of addresses for the main survey. This survey was also carried out by the Central Survey Unit of the Northern Ireland Statistics and Research Agency and fieldwork took place between October 2002 and January 2003. As with the Omnibus Survey, one household was selected at each address. One 'responsible' member of the household, the Household Respondent (HR), was asked a range of questions about the household, covering details of the household's income; the number of people; their age, employment status and other characteristics; and questions about the house and its condition. This was followed by individual interviews with all other people in the household

---

PSENI Survey II: Main Survey

Response Rate 64%

---

aged 16 or more. A household response rate of 64 per cent was achieved resulting in 1,976 household interviews and 3,104 individual interviews from a possible 3,865 persons.

The main survey also included a series of modules some of which were randomly assigned to half the individuals interviewed. The questions covered people's views on poverty, living standards within households, health and disability, neighbourhood characteristics, community support, activism, local services, mobility, 'the troubles', economic activity, income, finance and debt, and a self completion section covering views about health and economising behaviour (see Appendix).

Everyone in the household aged 16 and over was asked if they had the 90 necessities listed.

The interview was conducted with the aid of a small portable computer. Most of the questions were read from the computer by the interviewer and put to the person concerned. Where potentially sensitive questions were involved such as those on lack of necessities, identity, health and 'the troubles', the interviewee was handed the computer and asked to answer the questions as they appeared by touching the screen. This meant such questions could be answered entirely confidentially without the interviewer knowing the response. The questionnaire took between 60 and 90 minutes to complete.

Calculating the poverty threshold

Once the data had been collected in the manner outlined above, a poverty threshold was then calculated using the PSEB method. This involved a number of procedures, many of them technically complex. In summary the procedures tested the validity, reliability and additivity of indicators. First, those items defined as necessities by more than 50 per cent of the population in the first survey, but which were lacked by people because they could not afford them, were used as the basis for assessing the range of deprivation. This list of 40 items and activities can be considered 'politically' valid as a majority of the general public believe them to be necessities.

Table 3.1: *PSENI households in relation to deprivation items*

Number of items lacking	Number of households	Per cent	Cumulative Percent
0	1001	50.7	50.7
1	211	10.7	61.3
2	137	6.9	68.3
3	86	4.4	72.6
4	75	3.8	76.4
5	72	3.6	80.1
6	60	3.0	83.1
7	57	2.9	86.0
8	46	2.3	88.3
9	36	1.8	90.1
10	34	1.7	91.9
11	31	1.6	93.4
12	35	1.8	95.2
13	18	.9	96.1
14	13	.7	96.8
15	14	.7	97.5
16	11	.6	98.0
17	14	.7	98.7
18	7	.4	99.1
19	7	.4	99.4
20	4	.2	99.6
21	2	.1	99.7
22	3	.2	99.9
23	2	.1	100.0
Total	**1976**	**100.0**	**100.0**

Second, these items were tested to ascertain whether they were scientifically valid indicators of deprivation. 'Odds ratios' were calculated for each item compared to two indicators of poor health (Long Term Illness and a General Health Measure) and a subjective poverty measure. This process suggested that the following necessities were invalid: 'fridge', 'collecting children from school', 'visiting school', 'attending places of worship', 'television', 'dictionary', 'vacuum cleaner' and 'telephone'.

Third, the items were tested to ascertain whether they were reliable. In other words, if the measurement was repeated, would the same results be obtained? The statistical technique for this suggested that the following items were unreliable: 'visiting school', 'coach or train fares to visit friends/family', 'collecting children from school', 'health /disability aids', 'fridge', and 'television'. These two processes together suggested that eight items should be dropped from the computation of the poverty threshold because they were either invalid or unreliable, or both.

The fourth stage involved checking all the remaining items to ascertain whether they were additive. In other words, a household lacking two necessities should be better off than a household lacking four. This process further reduced the number of selected items from 32 to 29. The frequency counts of the number of these deprivation items lacked by households are shown in Table 3.1. Lack of necessities is very unevenly distributed. Most households lacked none or only one or two of the items. Half lacked no items, but a third however lacked three or more and a fifth six or more because they were unable to afford them. Seven per cent of households lacked twelve or more necessities.

Equivalising income

The fifth stage in calculating the poverty threshold involved analysis of household income. Although every individual in the household was asked for details of their income, the analysis reported here uses the total disposable household income estimated by the HR. Income data were not recorded by a tenth (190) of HRs. For these households an estimated income based on key household characteristics was imputed by the researchers. These respondents were about five years younger than others, more likely to be employed and more likely to be pensioner couples or members of larger families. They also reported lacking fewer necessities on average than others, suggesting that these respondents were generally better off than others. Despite imputing income to these cases, their non-reporting is likely to have lowered mean and median income levels in the survey findings as a whole, thereby slightly depressing poverty thresholds. Further analysis will be required to produce poverty thresholds based on the sum of individually reported incomes.

As noted in Chapter 1, household income was then subject to 'equivalisation'. This is a technical process designed to take account of differences in household composition so that, for example, the standard of living of a single person might reasonably be compared with a couple or a couple with children. A number of different equivalence scales are used in poverty research and measurement worldwide (see Chapter 5, Table 5.1).

Combining deprivation and income

The sixth and final step was to ascertain where the objective poverty threshold lay by examining the relationship between PSE equivalised income and the deprivation scores. Statistical techniques identified the combination of low income and lack of necessities which best distinguished between poor and non-poor households and maximised the similarities within each of these groups. Using a number of different methods, it emerged that the poverty threshold was at three items (or more) and that the average PSE equivalised income for poor households was £156.27 per week.

It is important to stress that the whole of the analysis presented in this report is based on equivalised household income. Where there are references to poor persons and individuals, these are people defined as poor by virtue of living in a poor household. Information on persons should be treated with caution for the obvious reason that not everyone living in a poor household is in fact themselves poor and certainly all members of a household are unlikely to be equally poor. Many adults, especially women, make personal sacrifices to ensure children are fed and clothed decently. Future work will explore the extent of poverty within households based on an analysis of income and deprivation for each individual in the household instead of an extrapolation based on the household.

Conclusion

People in Northern Ireland have broadly similar views on what constitute the bare necessities of life, as established in the first survey described in this study. The second, main survey looked at the extent to which households are deprived of the bare necessities as well as collecting data on a wide range of factors including income, employment, and social participation.

> **The Northern Ireland 2002/03 consensual poverty threshold:**
>
> Poor households are those that lack at least three deprivation items and have on average an equivalised income of £156.27 per week.

The PSE poverty threshold was established by combining the survey findings on deprivation and income, using a number of statistical procedures designed to best distinguish the 'poor' from the 'non-poor'. Poor households lack at least three deprivation items and have on average an equivalised household income of £156.27 per week.

The next chapter presents poverty figures for Northern Ireland based on the PSE method and compares them with poverty rates in Britain.

Chapter 4
Consensual Poverty in Northern Ireland

This chapter presents the figures on the extent of consensual poverty in Northern Ireland. The numbers above, below and around the poverty threshold are compared with those in Britain. The chapter begins with a brief examination of lack of necessities.

Adults necessities

Table 4.1 shows the ranked percentage of respondents identifying different adult items as necessities for each of seven domains, including food, housing and clothing. Forty of the 53 items were considered to be necessities by more than 50 per cent of the population. It is clear from these items that people interpret necessities in a broad way which goes beyond basic material items such as food, shelter and clothing. They also go beyond individual items, such as 'having a hobby or leisure activity' (82 per cent) and embrace a range of customary activities and social obligations. For example, 97 per cent of the population consider that 'visiting friends or family in hospital or other institutions' is a necessity. Similarly, 95 per cent consider 'celebrating special occasions such as Christmas' a necessity. A high proportion of the population consider other social obligations as necessities such as 'attending weddings, funerals or similar occasions' or 'family days out'.

Table 4.1 notes the proportion of people who say that they don't have or don't want the item, as well as the proportion of people who don't have and can't afford the item. There are two items that over 80 per cent of the population possess – a 'microwave oven' and 'video recorder' – but which are not considered to be necessities by the majority. This shows that there are goods which most people possess but which are not considered as essential for a basic standard of living.

Table 4.1:

Perception of adult necessities and how many people lack them (all figures show % of Household Respondents)

Key:

Italics – items regarded as 'necessary' by less than half of HRs.

Bold – items used to constuct the poverty index.

percentages	Omnibus 'Necessary'	Have	Don't have don't want	Can't afford
FOOD				
1 **Fresh fruit and vegetables every day**	92	84	11	5
2 **Meal with meat, chicken or fish every second day, if you wanted it**	83	90	7	3
3 **Roast dinner once a week**	59	86	11	3
HOUSING				
4 **Enough money to pay heating, electricity and telephone bills on time**	99	91	1	8
5 **Dry, damp free home**	98	92	4	4
6 **Health/disability aids and equipment, if needed**	98	43	53	4
7 **Enough money to keep your home in a decent state of decoration**	92	86	2	12
8 **Central heating**	84	94	3	3
9 **Replacing worn out furniture**	79	67	5	28
10 Second home/holiday home	*6*	*6*	*45*	*49*
CLOTHES				
11 **Warm, waterproof coat**	93	91	4	5
12 **Good clothes to wear for job interviews**	86	85	9	6
13 **Two pairs of strong shoes**	84	92	2	6
14 **Good outfit to wear for special occasions such as parties or weddings**	75	88	4	8
15 **New, not second hand clothes**	62	91	3	6
INFORMATION				
16 **Telephone (includes mobile)**	81	95	2	3
17 **Television**	71	98	1.5	0.5
18 **Dictionary**	61	84	15	1
19 Daily newspaper	*34*	*60*	*36*	*4*
20 Home computer	*20*	*47*	*38*	*15*
21 Access to the internet from home	*13*	*40*	*44*	*16*
22 Satellite/Cable T.V.	*7*	*42*	*41*	*17*
DURABLE GOODS				
23 **Fridge**	99	99	0.7	0.3
24 **Washing machine**	95	96	3	1
25 **Replacing/repairing broken electrical goods such as fridges or washing machines**	95	75	2	23
26 **Vacuum cleaner**	90	97	1	2
27 **Car**	53	71	17	12
28 **Deep freezer**	52	86	10	4
29 Microwave oven	*33*	*88*	*9*	*3*
30 Tumble dryer	*30*	*59*	*28*	*13*
31 Video recorder	*22*	*86*	*11*	*3*
32 Dishwasher	*12*	*38*	*46*	*16*
PERSONAL FINANCES				
33 **Access to a decent pension**	94	57	19	24
34 **Home contents insurance**	89	78	10	12
35 **Regular savings (of £10 per month) for rainy days or retirement**	83	64	8	28
36 **Small amount of money to spend each week on yourself, not on your family**	76	80	3	17
SOCIAL				
37 **Visiting friends or family in hospital or other institutions**	97	84	14	2
38 **Celebrating special occasions such as Christmas**	95	97	2.2	0.8
39 **Visiting friends or family locally**	91	92	7.1	0.9
40 **Attending weddings, funerals or similar occasions**	89	92	6	2
41 **Visiting school, for example for sports day, parents evening**	88	31	68.7	0.3
42 **Family days out**	86	74	19	7
43 **Collecting children from school**	84	21	78.4	0.6
44 **Having a hobby or leisure activity**	84	70	25	5
45 **Attending church or other place of religious worship**	75	66	33.5	0.5
46 **Presents for friends or family once a year**	72	87	2	11
47 **One weeks annual holiday away from home (not staying with relatives)**	60	57	19	24
48 **Visiting family/friends in other parts of the country by bus or train 4 times a year**	56	34	58	8
49 **Having friends or family visit for a drink or meal once a month**	52	62	28	10
50 Going out for evening meal once a fortnight	*40*	*45*	*39*	*16*
51 Going out for meal in a restaurant once a month	*35*	*53*	*28*	*19*
52 Pet, if you want one	*31*	*40*	*57*	*3*
53 Holiday abroad once a year	*19*	*34*	*31*	*35*

On the other hand, there are a number of items that over 80 per cent of the population believe are necessities, yet sizeable proportions of the population are unable to afford them. These include 'replacing worn out furniture', 'regular savings (of £10 per month) for rainy days or retirement' and 'access to a decent pension'. As we showed in Chapter 3, lack of necessities is very unevenly distributed with half lacking no items and 7 per cent twelve or more.

Consensual poverty

Using the consensual mixed income-deprivation method described in Chapter 3, well over a quarter of Northern Ireland's households – 29.6 per cent – were poor in 2002/03. A further 2.1 per cent of households were judged to have recently risen out of poverty – that is they lacked three or more necessities but had relatively high incomes. Another 12.1 per cent could be described as vulnerable to poverty in that their incomes were relatively low but they did not currently lack three or more necessities. When these two groups are excluded, it means that there are 185,500 poor households in Northern Ireland. There are 502,200 people living in these poor households and 148,900 of these are children.

Figure 4.1: *Household poverty rates, PSENI and PSEB compared*

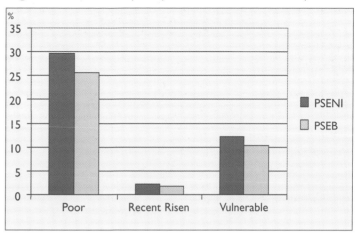

185,500 households
are poor

502,200 people
live in poor households

148,900 children
are living in poor households

Table 4.2: *Views of children's necessities and proportions lacking children's necessities.*

percentages	Omnibus 'Necessary'	Main Survey Have	Main Survey Don't have don't want	Main Survey Can't afford
FOOD				
1 Fresh fruit or vegetables at least once a day	97	89	7	(4)
2 Three meals a day	95	96	3	(1)
3 Meat, fish or vegetarian equivalent at least twice a day	80	87	8	5
CLOTHES				
4 New, properly fitted shoes	99	97	1	(2)
5 Warm waterproof coat or jacket	98	95	2	(3)
6 All the school uniform required by the school*	95	86	13	(1)
7 Buy new clothes when needed	92	91	1	8
8 At least seven pairs of new underpants	83	93	3	(4)
9 At least four pairs of trousers, leggings or skirts	84	95	1	(4)
10 At least four warm tops, such as jumpers, fleeces or sweatshirts	93	95	1	(4)
11 New, not second-hand clothes	70	92	0	8
PARTICIPATION and ACTIVITIES				
12 Opportunity to take regular exercise	97	95	4	(1)
13 Celebrations on special occasions	95	98	1	(1)
14 Hobby/leisure activity*	94	78	18	4
15 School trip at least once a term*	92	84	14	(2)
16 Family day trips	89	84	6	10
17 Youth club or similar activity	88	59	37	(4)
18 Sports gear or equipment	76	80	12	8
19 One week's holiday away from home with family	69	64	8	28
20 Friends round to visit*	72	82	16	(2)
21 Going to the cinema regularly	*25*	*60*	*25*	*15*
DEVELOPMENTAL				
22 Books of their own	92	97	2	(1)
23 Play group (pre-school age)*	87	58	39	(3)
24 Educational games	86	88	7	5
25 Toys (e.g. dolls, play figures etc.)*	88	95	4.6	(0.4)
26 Construction toys such as Lego	72	77	19	(4)
27 Bicycle*	54	79	14	7
28 At least 50 pence per week pocket money	82	78	18	(4)
29 Computer suitable for doing school work	56	63	16	21
30 Comic, or magazine once a week	52	57	32	11
31 Pet, if wanted	*40*	*49*	*46*	*5*
32 Computer games	*21*	*64*	*21*	*15*
33 Access to the internet from home	*20*	*49*	*27*	*24*
ENVIRONMENTAL				
54 Health/disability aids and equipment, if needed	99	52	45	(3)
35 Their own bed	94	97	2	(1)
36 Enough bedrooms for boys and girls over 10 to sleep separately*	87	86	7	7
37 Garden to play in	76	89	6	5

Key:

Italics – items regarded as 'necessary' by less than half of HRs;
Brackets ( ) – less than 20 unweighted cases;
* – age-related items.

While the PSEB and PSENI data were gathered three years apart, it is still useful to compare their results. Northern Ireland's poverty rate in 2002/03 was four percentage points above that in Britain in 1999 (Figure 4.1).

Children's necessities

A particular focus of UK policy since 1998 has been children's poverty and the remainder of this chapter focuses on children's poverty in Northern Ireland. Adults in the PSENI were asked to identify necessities for children as well as adults. Table 4.2 lists the 37 items and activities adults were asked about, organised into five domains. Only four items were not regarded as necessities by the majority of adults. More than ten children's items attracted a consensus of over 90 per cent. These included 'new, properly fitted shoes' (99 per cent), 'warm waterproof coat or jacket' (98 per cent), 'three meals a day' (95 per cent) 'their own bed' (94 per cent) and 'books of their own' (92 per cent). In the main survey, the parent nominated as most likely to know about the children's standard of living was identified and answered questions about children's necessities – see Table 4.2.

As with adult items, there was a broad correspondence between what people considered to be necessities and how likely these items were to be owned. Two of the items which were not believed to be necessities for

Living standard vignettes

The vignettes below and on the following pages give a brief description of the economic circumstances and living conditions of PSE-defined poor households. The names are fictitious but the commentaries are based on real profiles of respondents to the PSENI survey. The average equivalised weekly income of poor households was £156.27.

Vignette 1
Widowed pensioner

Mary is a pensioner aged 67 with a weekly income of £95 per week (or £136 equivalised). She is widowed and lives alone in a property rented from the Housing Executive.

She thinks her neighbourhood is a very good place to live and people are friendly. However, she does not have enough money to keep her home in a decent state of decoration. She doesn't have home contents insurance because she can't afford to. She would like to replace worn out furniture and to replace or repair broken electrical goods, but can't afford to do so.

Mary economises a lot by buying cheaper cuts of meat and cutting back on telephone calls to family and friends. In fact she 'often' uses less gas, electricity and telephone than she needs to and she worries about household finances 'all the time'. However, she does visit friends and family, and while she doesn't have a car, she finds it easy to get about using public transport.

children were nonetheless owned by over 60 per cent of children.

The item lacked by the greatest majority of children was 'One week's holiday a year away from home with family' (28 per cent). A very similar proportion of adults reported the same enforced lack (24 per cent, see Table 4.1). Eight per cent of households with children were reported to rely on second hand clothing.

The extent of child poverty in Northern Ireland

One way to measure the extent of child poverty is to count up the number of children living in poor households. On this basis 37.4 per cent of all children (aged 15 or under) in Northern Ireland are growing up in households falling below the consensual poverty threshold. This means that 148,900 children live in such households.

This approach makes two important assumptions, which may not be true. First, it assumes that if the household is poor then the children are also poor. Second, it assumes that the lack of items and activities for adults applies similarly to children. Neither may be the case because resources are not evenly distributed within households. It may therefore be more appropriate to use children's items and activities together with low income as the basis of determining the child poverty

---

Vignette 2

Lone parent with young child

Sarah is in her late 30s, separated from her husband and living alone with her seven year old year son in private rented accommodation. She is currently behind with her rent and can't afford to insure the contents of her home.

Sarah's weekly income is £130 (or £113 equivalised). She worries about her household finances all the time and is very dissatisfied with her standard of living. She feels that she lacks adequate heating and sometimes puts up with feeling cold or stays in bed to save on heating costs. She can't afford to buy fresh fruit and vegetables for herself and her son everyday, nor does she have any money to spend on herself. When furniture wears out or electrical goods break down, she is unable to replace them. She has had to keep wearing old clothes because she can't afford to buy new ones. She would like to have a holiday once a year but can't afford to. Nor can she afford to buy her son a weekly comic or magazine. Sarah's health is poor as she suffers from quite severe asthma and depression and takes medication for both. Her mobility and ability to do housework are limited 'quite a lot'.

Sarah likes where she lives, but feels that she doesn't have any influence on decisions taken about the area. She lives in a 'friendly' neighbourhood and sees it as a place where local people look after each other.

Vignette 3

Couple with three children

Margaret and Sean live in a Housing Executive terrace house in a small town. Margaret has no job and spends her time looking after the children aged 15, 10 and 7. Sean suffers from a disability and has not worked for eight years. Their household income is less than £200 a week (or less than £100 equivalised) including child benefit. They are very dissatisfied with their current standard of living and worry about money all the time. They have central heating, but don't have enough money to pay heating and other bills on time. They can't make regular savings for rainy days or retirement and neither has a pension. They do not have two pairs of strong shoes or a good outfit to wear to special occasions such as parties or weddings. They can't afford holidays or a range of other social activities. They can't afford house contents insurance.

The children don't have construction toys such as lego or any educational games and they do not possess at least four pairs of trousers, leggings, jeans or jogging bottoms. None of the children have a hobby or a leisure activity and they don't go to the cinema regularly or to a youth club and they do not have friends around for tea. There is no money for any of these activities.

The family have been badly affected by the 'troubles'. Three close relatives have been killed and they know others who have been killed. Moreover, they were forced to move house because of intimidation.

Vignette 4

Lone parent with adult son

Joan is divorced and lives with her 23 year old son. She works for the health service and has an income of £170 per week (or £148 equivalised). She is the only person working in the household. The property is mortgaged and is in her name only.

She would like to decorate her home and replace or repair broken electrical goods but she can't afford to. She has often bought second hand clothes and relied on gifts of clothing. She doesn't have a warm waterproof coat or two pairs of strong shoes and she would like to have a small amount of money to spend on herself.

Joan worries about finances all the time and has often skimped on food so that her son would have enough to eat. She doesn't have a car but visits family and friends using public transport. She also has friends round to visit at least once a month.

threshold and hence the number of children in poverty, but such a calculation has not been carried out for this report.

Conclusion

The PSE method reveals that half of all households are deprived of no items regarded as basic necessities by the majority of people in Northern Ireland. Two thirds lack no items or just one or two. When combined with income, well over a quarter of households are poor as defined by the PSE method. These households contain over half a million people, including almost 150,000 children.

How these figures compare with other measures of poverty and low income is explored in the next chapter.

Chapter 5
Relative Income and Consistent Poverty Measures

This chapter examines the extent of poverty in Northern Ireland when compared with the HBAI series for Great Britain and the latest Living in Ireland survey. The chapter begins with a discussion of income equivalisation because each of these measures uses a different equivalence scale. Most of the comparisons which follow are based on relative income, with the exception of the Republic of Ireland's consistent poverty measure which combines relative income with deprivation of one of eight basic necessities. The chapter concludes with a discussion of income inequality.

Equivalence scales

A number of equivalence scales are used in poverty research and measurement. Four of these are shown in Table 5.1. The HBAI uses the McClements scale; the 'before housing costs' weights used are shown in Table 5.1 while Eurostat comparisons for EU countries are calculated using the 'modified OECD' scale. The Republic of Ireland (A) equivalisation scale is based on the levels of social welfare benefits payable in the Irish Republic. The scale used in PSEB was devised using the results of budget standards research. It gives more weight to children than the McClements scale (see Bradshaw, 1993; and Middleton *et al*, 1997).

The modified OECD and Republic of Ireland (A) scales weight the first adult as 1.0 whereas PSEB and McClements weight the first adult plus spouse as 1.0. This means that PSEB and McClements are on a similar basis and can be compared, and likewise OECD and Republic of Ireland (A).

The impact of the different equivalence scales as applied to the PSENI household incomes is shown in Table 5.2. With no equivalisation, average weekly household income was £370.10. Using the McClements equivalence scale, average weekly household income was £343.90. As HBAI now presents low-income

Table 5.1: *Weightings used in equivalence scales*

	PSE[1]	McClements[2]	Modified OECD	RoI
First Adult	0.70	0.61	1.0	1.00
Spouse	0.30	0.39	0.5	0.66
Other Second Adult	0.45	0.46	0.5	0.66
Third Adult	0.45	0.42	0.5	0.66
Subsequent Adults	0.45	0.36	0.5	0.66
Children aged under 14yrs	0.35	0.20	0.3	0.33
Children aged 14yrs and over	0.30	0.30	0.5	0.33

Notes

1. The PSE scale weights the first child at 0.35 and each additional child at 0.3. If the head of the household is a lone parent 0.1 is added.
2. The McClements scale has more age groups than shown above: 0-1 = 0.09; 2-4 = 0.18; 5-7 = 0.21; 8-10 = 0.23; 11-12 = 0.25; 13-15 = 0.27; 16 and over = 0.36.

Table 5.2: *Mean and Median PSENI Equivalised Incomes (£ per week)*

	Not equivalised	Equivalence scale			
		PSE	McClements	Modified OECD	Republic of Ireland
Mean	370.1	304.8	343.9	221.3	205.7
Median	290.0	236.4	270.0	170.0	162.2

Table 5.3: *Proportion of PSENI households (and persons living in those households) with incomes below relative income thresholds*

Percentages Households N = 1976 (Persons N = 5163)	Equivalence scale			
	PSE	Modified OECD	McClements	Republic of Ireland
<70% Median	32.1 (32.3)	30.1 (28.8)	30.9 (29.5)	31.0 (30.6)
<60% Median	24.1 (24.7)	22.9 (21.8)	23.5 (21.6)	23.7 (23.2)
<50% Median	16.4 (17.3)	14.1 (13.8)	14.6 (14.1)	14.6 (14.1)
<60% Mean	35.6 (36.9)	35.9 (34.7)	34.4 (33.5)	34.6 (35.1)
<50% Mean	26.9 (27.8)	27.1 (25.3)	25.7 (23.2)	26.7 (26.7)
<40% Mean	17.5 (18.1)	16.3 (15.7)	14.9 (14.3)	15.4 (15.3)

statistics for persons rather than households, it is necessary to calculate mean and median incomes on an individual rather than household basis in order to provide the appropriate comparison. The average equivalised weekly income for individuals was £337.95. The equivalent figure in Great Britain (GB) for 2001/2 was £384 (Department for Work and Pensions, 2003a: 11). The GB HBAI median was £311, compared with a Northern Ireland figure of £268.97 for 2002.

The higher the equivalised income, the less 'generous' the scale and the less likely a particular household will be defined as having a low income or as falling below a poverty threshold. As previously noted, the PSE scale can be compared with McClements, and the modified OECD with the Republic of Ireland (A) scale. The latter is 6-7 per cent more generous than the modified OECD scale, and the PSEB is about 10 per cent more generous than the McClements scale (see Table 5.2).

Using the four equivalence scales, the PSENI household income data were used to calculate proportions of households (and persons in those households) living below a range of relative income thresholds. The results are shown in Table 5.3. The PSE scale generally captures a higher proportion of households below the thresholds. For example, 24.1 per cent of households (476) have incomes below 60per cent of median income using the PSE equivalence scale. The modified OECD scale produces the lowest figures for this threshold (22.9 per cent, or 452 households) – resulting in 24 fewer households below the threshold.

The proportion of persons (shown in brackets in Table 5.3), as opposed to households, living below the equivalised household income thresholds tends to be higher under the PSE scale because of the heavier weightings for children.

Figure 5.1 charts the data in Table 5.3, selecting the two most commonly used relative income lines – 50 per cent of mean household income and 60 per cent of the median income. It shows the proportions of persons living in households below each of these thresholds.

Irish comparisons: consistent and overall poverty measures

As discussed in Chapter 2, two key measures of poverty are used in the Republic of Ireland, 'consistent' and 'overall' poverty. Using the same Republic of Ireland (A) equivalence scale, a consistent poverty measure was computed for Northern Ireland using less than 60 per cent mean income and enforced lack of at least one of the eight items which make up the Republic of Ireland basic

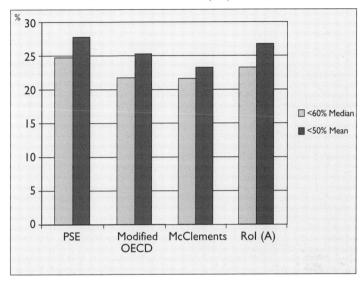

Figure 5.1: *Proportion of persons living in PSENI households below 60% median and 50% mean incomes by equivalence scale*

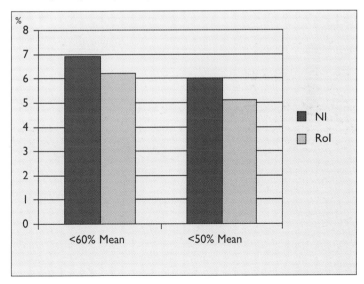

Figure 5.2: *Households in consistent poverty, PSENI and Living in Ireland (2000) surveys compared*

Figure 5.3: *Proportion of persons below median income thresholds (Northern Ireland and Republic of Ireland)*

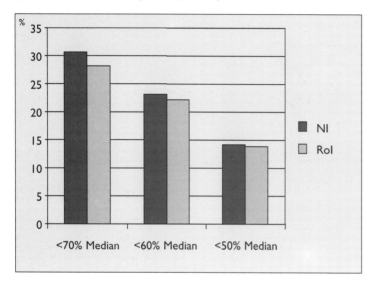

Figure 5.4: *Proportion of households below mean income thresholds (Northern Ireland and Republic of Ireland)*

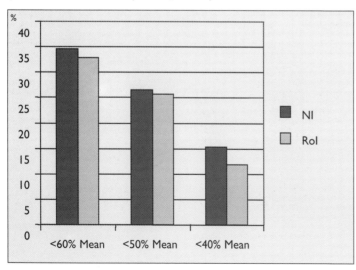

deprivation index. On this basis, 6.9 per cent of households in Northern Ireland are in 'consistent poverty'.

Figure 5.2 shows the marginal variation in consistent poverty rates as between Northern Ireland and the Republic of Ireland, bearing in mind the time gap in data collection (two years). It is perhaps surprising that consistent poverty rates between the two do not differ more given growth rates in the Republic of Ireland economy over the last ten years. However, unemployment and 'inactivity' rates north and south were steadily converging throughout the 1990s and were much the same by 2000 (Tomlinson, 2001).

The second measure of poverty used in the Republic of Ireland is 'overall poverty', which is a simple measure of relative income. Again, using the Republic of Ireland (A) scale, the proportions of persons living in households with incomes below the range of thresholds reported for the Republic of Ireland are shown in Figure 5.3. Again, the rates are very similar. At the below 70 per cent median threshold, 28.2 per cent of persons live in poor households in the Republic of Ireland compared with 30.6 per cent in Northern Ireland, a figure also very close to the PSENI consensual household poverty rate of 29.6 per cent.

Figure 5.4 compares relative income levels using proportions of the mean, rather than the median. The differences between Northern Ireland and the Republic of Ireland are less using this measure, except at the 40 per cent of mean threshold where the difference is 3.6 percentage points.

Britain and Northern Ireland comparisons: HBAI based measures

Figures 5.5 and 5.6 present Britain and Northern Ireland comparisons based on the proportions of persons living in poor households using the HBAI method and equivalisation scale. On all median measures (Figure 5.5) Northern Ireland has higher 'poverty' rates than Great Britain, generally 5 percentage points higher. A similar result for mean income thresholds is shown in Figure 5.6, although these means may not be strictly comparable because the HBAI series adjusts very high incomes in a way that could not be reproduced and was arguably inappropriate for the PSENI data.

Northern Ireland compared

The analyses above have shown that poverty rates in Northern Ireland are higher than in Great Britain and the Republic of Ireland. Whichever poverty measure is selected for Northern Ireland, significant proportions of

Figure 5.5: *Proportion of persons living in households below HBAI median income thresholds (Northern Ireland and Great Britain)*

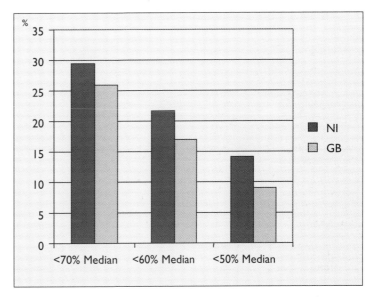

Figure 5.6: *Proportion of persons living below HBAI mean income thresholds (Northern Ireland and Great Britain)*

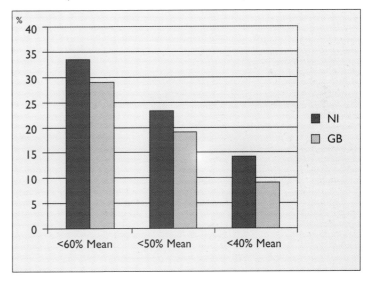

Figure 5.7: *Northern Ireland poverty rates, using different methods of calculation (proportions of persons)*

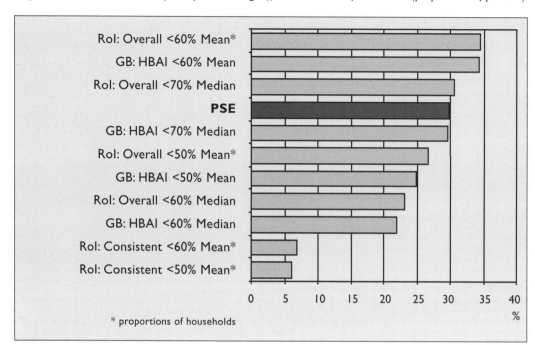

households and people are living in poverty (see Figure 5.7).

Inequality

There is a growing volume of evidence which suggests that while poverty blights lives and leads to health and other social problems, what is more important is the extent of inequality, the gap between rich and the poor (Shaw *et al*, 1999). A number of robust health studies have shown that the more unequal the distribution of income the greater the chances of people getting sick and dying young. Two important studies comparing the 50 states in the USA (Kaplan *et al*, 1996; Kennedy *et al*, 1996) showed that not only did greater disparities in income lead to greater death rates but they were also associated with other social problems such as a higher proportion of babies born with low birth rates, higher murder and violent crime rates, and higher proportions of people not being able to work because of disability. At the same time, states with the greatest inequality had higher costs per head on medical care and law and order. Although not examining the association between death rates and inequality, a recent study of mortality in Ireland showed considerable disparities in life expectancy between different sections of the population. In particular, in both the North and the South, the all-causes mortality rate in the lowest occupational class was 100-200 per cent higher than the rate in the highest occupational class (Balanda, 2001).

There are a number of different ways of analysing the extent of inequality. One simple way is to consider the distribution of income. Figure 5.8 shows the income distribution for the total population in Northern Ireland equivalised by the McClements scale and hence comparable with the distribution published annually in the HBAI series for Great Britain. The shaded areas numbered 1 to 10 show each successive tenth, or decile of the population. The distribution, like the GB distribution, is clearly skewed towards the lower end and has a long

Figure 5.8: *Income distribution (McClements equivalised) of total Northern Ireland population 2002/2003*

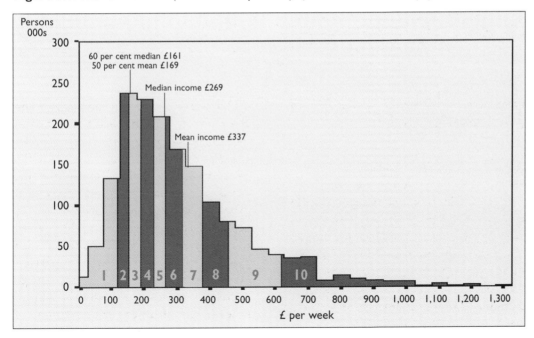

tail at the upper end. Over 64 per cent of individuals had an equivalised income that was less than the national average, compared with 60 per cent in Britain. As can be seen from the figure, there was a heavy concentration of individuals around the 50 per cent of the mean income and 60 per cent of the median points.

Another way to consider inequality is to take two points on the income distribution – the 90th percentile and the 10th percentile – and divide the former by the later. Using the PSENI data, in 2002/2003 this ratio was 5.21 for Northern Ireland. This means that rich individuals received five times the income of poor individuals. Data from the Family Expenditure Survey in 1988 gave the same ratio as 3.63 showing a very considerable increase in income inequality in Northern Ireland over the last fifteen years (McGregor and McKee, 1995).

A more widely used measure of inequality is the Gini coefficient. This measures the extent to which the distribution of income deviates from a perfectly equal distribution. It can be used to show disparities in income as well as other social phenomena such as inequality in education. A Lorenz curve is used to plot the cumulative distribution of total income which people receive against the cumulative number of people who receive the

Table 5.4: *Family Expenditure Survey and PSENI Gini Coefficients compared*

Year/survey	Gini coefficient	Numbers of Households
1998/99 FES	38	600
1999/00 FES	36	586
2000/01 FES	39	524
2002/03 PSENI	42	1976

income starting with the poorest. The Gini coefficient measures the area between the curve and a hypothetical line of absolute equality. It is typically expressed as a percentage and runs on a scale of 0, representing total equality, to 100, representing total inequality or where one person gets all the income.

Using PSENI data, the Gini coefficent for Northern Ireland is 42 per cent. A recent study (McClelland and Gribbin, 2002) calculated the Gini coefficients for various years, based on PSE equivalised income, using the Family Expenditure Survey (FES). The results are shown in Table 5.4.

The data also suggest that inequality in Northern Ireland is increasing. Although international comparisons are difficult because of different timescales and methods, nevertheless, they help to put Northern Ireland in context. Based on the 2002/2003 figure, Northern Ireland is one of the most unequal societies in the developed world.

More recently another method of considering inequality has been developed (Kennedy *et al*, 1996). It is called the Robin Hood index. It is calculated by dividing the population into 10 equal groups from the richest to the poorest and then calculating which group's income exceeds 10 per cent of the total income and by what percentage. The percentages of all the groups in excess are then summed and the product of the number of 10 per cent groups, which meet this criterion, subtracted. It is expressed in percentage terms and therefore the higher the percentage the greater the inequality. Using McClements equivalised net household income for the total population in Northern Ireland, the Robin Hood Index comes to 27 per cent. Put another way, the top four income groups together possess 67 per cent of the total household income in Northern Ireland. Yet to achieve total income equality they should have only 40 per cent of the income. Thus 27 per cent of the income would have to be redistributed from these top four deciles to the bottom six groups in order to achieve equality.

Conclusion

On all measures presented in this chapter, Northern Ireland has higher poverty rates than the Republic of Ireland and Great Britain, though the differences are marginal in the case of the Republic of Ireland. The scale of poverty is a reflection of widening income inequalities. Northern Ireland is not only characterised by high poverty levels but also by considerably higher levels of income inequality than Britain.

The next chapter considers who the poor are in terms of the key dimensions of inequality.

Chapter 6
Equality and Consensual Poverty

As noted in Chapter 1, one of the aims of the research was to examine how poverty and social exclusion varied across the nine dimensions of equality specified in Section 75 of the 1998 Northern Ireland Act. Poverty rates for people on either side of these various dimensions are shown in this chapter to vary considerably from the overall consensual poverty rate of 29.6 per cent.

In the following analysis, the characteristics of the household respondent are the basis of the presentation, except for gender and disability where the total numbers of men and women within households are considered. For example, a 'Protestant household' is defined by the nominal religion of the household respondent.

The first part of this chapter examines the position of households and individuals within them across the nine equality dimensions. Each of the graphs shows a number of things. First,

Section 75 equality duty

A public authority shall in carrying out its functions relating to Northern Ireland have due regard to the need to promote equality of opportunity –

a) between persons of different religious belief, political opinion, racial group, age, marital status or sexual orientation;

b) between men and women generally;

c) between persons with a disability and persons without; and

d) between persons with dependants and persons without.

bar charts are used to show poverty rates for different sub-groups within the chosen dimension. Second, pie charts display the share of poverty for each sub-group within the dimension. Thus in respect of marital status,

Figure 6.1: *Poverty rate by 'religion' of HR*

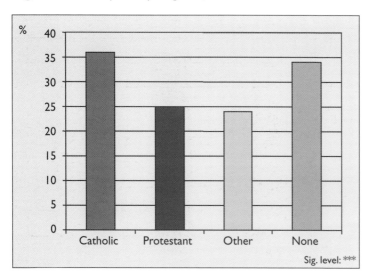

Statistical significance

It is possible to calculate the probability that the results reflect a real underlying difference between the different categories in the sample or simply chance. These calculations are called tests of significance and are traditionally calculated at either the 95 per cent or the 99 per cent confidence level. Thus, at the 95 per cent confidence level, we can be 95 per cent certain that the results are not due to chance.

Significance levels are shown as follows: * < 0.05, ** <0.01, *** <0.001

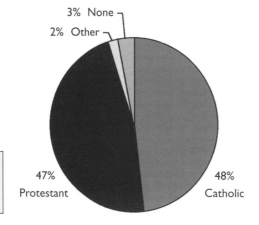

Figure 6.1a:
Share of poverty by 'religion' of HR

in poverty (see the marital status pie chart). The graphs also note whether the differences shown are statistically significant.

Religion

Poverty is a major problem along a number of Section 75 equality dimensions. Taking religious affiliation first, 36 per cent of Catholic households are in poverty compared with 25 per cent of Protestant households. Both groups however make up similar proportions of poor households – 47 per cent of poor households are Protestant and 48 per cent Catholic (Figure 6.1a)

widowed people have a poverty rate around the average 28 per cent (see the marital status bar chart) and they constitute only 11 per cent of all those

National Identity

When examined in terms of national identity, the proportions experiencing poverty appear to mirror the poverty rates by religious affiliation. Thirty seven per cent of 'Irish' households are poor compared with 25 per cent of 'British' households. Meanwhile, British households form almost the same proportion as Protestant households in poverty at 49 per cent, while Irish households form 33 per cent. This suggests that a sizeable proportion of Catholics define themselves as 'other' rather than 'Irish' in terms of national identity (Figures 6.2 and 6.2a).

Figure 6.2: *Poverty rate by national identity of HR*

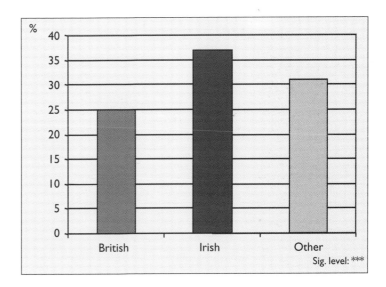

Sig. level: ***

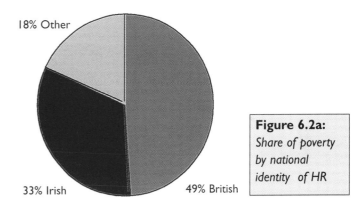

Figure 6.2a: *Share of poverty by national identity of HR*

Figure 6.3: *Poverty rate by political opinion of HR*

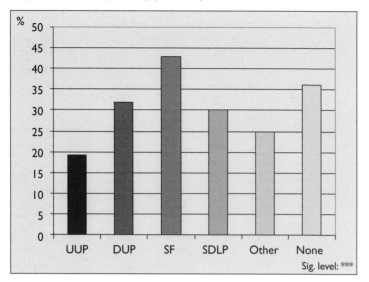

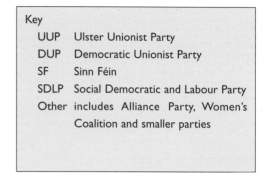

Key

UUP	Ulster Unionist Party
DUP	Democratic Unionist Party
SF	Sinn Féin
SDLP	Social Democratic and Labour Party
Other	includes Alliance Party, Women's Coalition and smaller parties

Figure 6.3a: *Share of poverty by political opinion of HR*

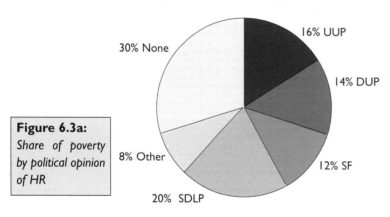

Political Opinion

Poverty rates vary much more between people who express different political party preferences. Some 43 per cent of households in which the HR's political preference was for Sinn Féin were poor compared with 19 per cent of those in which the HR's political preference was for the Ulster Unionist Party (see Figure 6.3). Poverty rates for supporters of the Democratic Unionist Party were however above average (at 32 per cent), while the SDLP's were average (at 30 per cent).

Figure 6.3a shows that almost a third (30 per cent) of HRs in poor households stated no political preference. The Democratic Unionist Party and Sinn Féin shares of poverty appear lower than expected, given real voting patterns and the poverty rates shown in Figure 6.3, and should be treated with caution.

Age

Looking at different age bands, younger household respondents were more likely to be poor with some 41 per cent of households in poverty where the household respondent was aged 16-24. Households with the lowest poverty rate (22 per cent) were those where the HR was aged 75 plus (see Figure 6.4). This may reflect the way current living standards reflect past as well as present incomes.

Figure 6.4: *Poverty rate by age of HR*

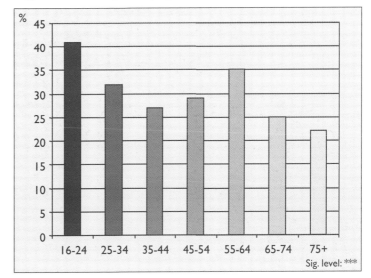

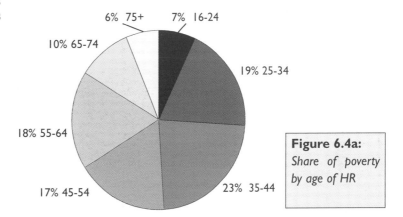

Figure 6.4a: *Share of poverty by age of HR*

Figure 6.5: *Poverty rate by marital status of HR*

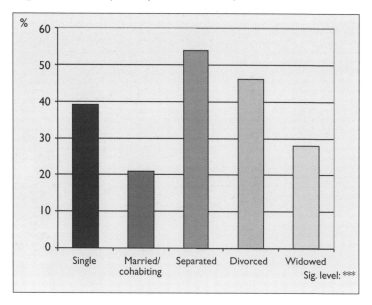

Marital status

The marital status of household respondents is strongly associated with poverty. Households where the respondent is separated have the highest rate of poverty (54 per cent), followed by those who are divorced (46 per cent) and then single people (39 per cent). Only those who are married or cohabiting have a poverty rate below the average (Figure 6.5).

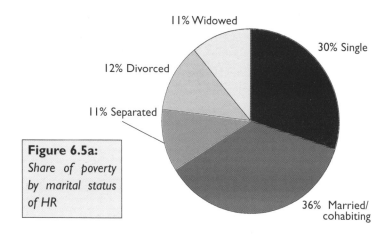

Figure 6.5a: *Share of poverty by marital status of HR*

Gender

There are significance differences between men and women. A quarter (25 per cent) of men live in poor households while 29 per cent of women do so (Figure 6.6). In terms of the share of poverty, 57 per cent of adults in poor households are women. Poverty is clearly a gender issue.

Disability and ill health

Households with one or more disabled members are more likely than others to be in poverty. Over half (56 per cent) of households containing one or more disabled people are in poverty compared with 29 per cent containing no one with a disability (Figure 6.7). Households which reported having at least one member with a disability however made up only 6 per cent of all those in poverty.

When respondents were however asked if they had a 'Long-term illness, health problem or disability which limits daily activities or work you can do', those who answered 'yes' were half of all those in poverty and had a poverty rate of 42 per cent. There may then have been some under-reporting of disability by survey respondents in poor households.

Figure 6.6: *Poverty rate by gender of adults in poor households*

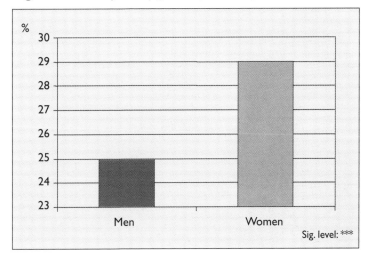

Figure 6.7: *Poverty rate of households with disabled people*

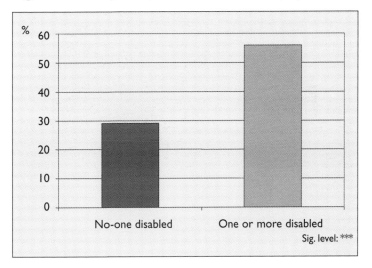

Figure 6.8: *Poverty rate by households with or without dependants*

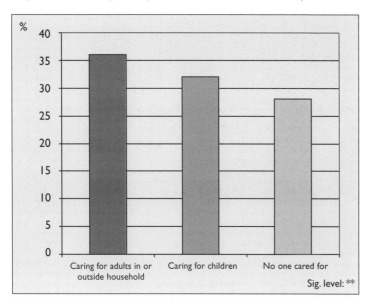

Sig. level: **

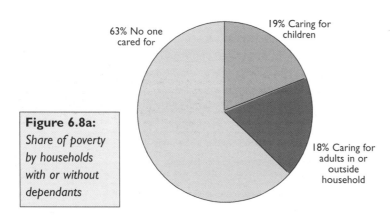

Figure 6.8a: *Share of poverty by households with or without dependants*

Carers

One of the section 75 dimensions is having or not having dependants. For the purposes of this analysis, having dependants was defined either as living with children under 16 in the household or as providing unpaid help and assistance to another adult whether in the same or another household. Childless households in which one adult was caring for another adult, in their own household or elsewhere, had a poverty rate of 36 per cent and made up 18 per cent of all households in poverty. Households caring for children were 19 per cent of all households in poverty and had a poverty rate of 32 per cent (Figure 6.8).

'Race' and sexual orientation

The final two dimensions of Section 75 are 'race' and sexual orientation. Only 16 (0.8 per cent) HRs belonged to ethnic minorities and had a low poverty rate (19 per cent), but this cannot be regarded as reliable or significant.

Similarly, the figures for sexual orientation are not significant or reliable. Two dozen HRs stated that they preferred same sex relationships and 16 said they were bisexual. The poverty rates for these two groups were 48 and 44 per cent respectively.

Other

There are a number of other ways of categorising households which are not specified under Section 75, but where high rates of poverty are demonstrable. These include:

	per cent
Lone parents	67
Housing Executive tenants	67
HRs with no qualifications	43
Workless households – sick/disabled	100
Workless households – unemployed	70

Subjective experiences of poverty

As well as developing an objective definition of poverty based on lack of necessities and income, it is possible to utilise people's own definition of their circumstances. Everyone in the survey was asked: How many pounds a week, after tax, do you think are necessary to keep a household, such as the one you live in, out of poverty? People were then asked: How far above or below that level would you say your household is? The results given by the HRs are shown in Table 6.1.

The results show that a subjective definition of poverty corresponds to a certain extent with an objective definition and is statistically significant. Of those who claim that their household income is about the same as the poverty income they

Table 6.1: *Subjective and consensual measures of poverty compared*

How far above or below the nominated poverty level?	Poverty rate	Share of poverty
A lot above that level	3	1
A little above that level	7	6
About the same	23	21
A little below that level	53	33
A lot below that level	82	39
		sig. level: ***

Table 6.2: *Extent of borrowing and poverty*

Source of borrowing for day-to-day needs	Poverty rate	Share of poverty	sig. level
Pawnbroker	63	1	n/s
Money lender	89	5	***
Friends	79	11	***
Family	72	27	***
None of these	23	59	***

Table 6.3: *Views on adequacy of income*

Thinking about your income, how adequate is it to meet your basic needs?	Poverty rate	Share of poverty
More than enough	2	2
Just enough	24	42
Not enough	72	56
		sig. level: ***

Table 6.4: *Poverty over time*

Looking back over your life, have there been times when you think you have lived in poverty by the standards of that time?	Poverty rate	Share of poverty
Never	15	23
Rarely	27	11
Occasionally	38	34
Often	53	24
Most of the time	71	8
		sig. level: ***

stated, some 23 per cent are in poverty. Of those who are a little below, some 53 per cent are in poverty and of those who claim they are a lot below, 82 per cent are in poverty. Conversely, of the people who believed their income was a lot above the level needed to keep their household out of poverty, 97 per cent were not poor.

Poverty rates are also associated with measures of financial stress such as debt and borrowing for every day needs. Of those who had used a moneylender, 89 per cent were poor and the poverty rate of those who had borrowed money from friends was 79 per cent (Table 6.2). On the other hand 59 per cent of poor households said they had not borrowed from any of the sources listed.

HRs were also asked to assess the adequacy of their household incomes relative to their needs. Some 24 per cent of HRs who thought that it was just enough were in poverty. Of those who thought that it was not enough some 72 per cent were in poverty (Table 6.3). Yet 42 per cent of poor households said they had 'just enough' to meet basic needs.

The dynamics of poverty over time can also be assessed subjectively. People were asked two biographical questions. The first asked them to look back over their lives, and state whether they had ever lived in poverty. If they believed they had they were asked a follow-up question about whether this was when they were a child or an adult or both. Of those HRs who believed that they had been living in poverty 'most of the time', 71 per cent were currently living in poverty (Table 6.4). Twenty-three per cent of those households counted as poor on the PSE consensual measure, however, reported they had never lived in poverty.

Dignan (2003) using Continuous Household Survey (CHS) data found that between 1990/91 and 2001/02 in Northern Ireland three types of households became significantly more prominent in the bottom 30 per cent of the income distribution. The three types of households were lone parent families, households headed by a sick or disabled person and sole earner couples with children. This suggests that relationship breakdown, job loss on the part of a family's second earner and the acquisition or continuance of ill health or disability are all life events which affect movements into and out of poverty and low income.

The second question on dynamics asked if anything had happened in the last two years which had improved or reduced their standard of living. Of those HRs who said that something had happened recently which reduced either their standard of living or their income, 52 per cent and 37 per cent, respectively, were living in poverty. Significantly, those who said that

Table 6.5: *Life events and change in standard of living*

Has anything happened recently (in the last two years) in your life which has... ?	Poverty rate	Share of poverty
Improved your standard of living	20	7
Reduced your standard of living	52	15
Increased your income	20	7
Reduced your icome	37	16
None of these	28	55

nothing had happened made up 55 per cent of all households living in poverty (Table 6.5).

Conclusion

There are striking differences in poverty rates when different dimensions of inequality are considered. Of all persons in poor households, 57 per cent are female. Divorced and separated HRs have the highest risk of poverty while married or cohabiting HRs have the lowest. Half of poor households are characterised by long-term limiting illness, health problems or disability, and carers have higher than average poverty rates. A quarter of Protestant households are in poverty, compared with over a third (36 per cent) of Catholic households. In terms of political preference almost one third of DUP supporters are in poverty while SDLP supporters have an average poverty rate. The most striking contrast is that the poverty rate for Sinn Féin supporters is 2.26 times that of Ulster Unionist Party supporters.

People in poor households do not necessarily see themselves as poor, although two-thirds of the poor think they have been poor 'occasionally', 'often' or 'most of the time' when they look back over their lives.

Chapter 7
Social Exclusion

This chapter reports on a number of aspects of social exclusion. How to eradicate social exclusion and increase inclusion was the subject of a detailed report for the Civic Forum in 2002 (Civic Forum, 2002). For the purposes of this study, social exclusion was explored along six main dimensions: exclusion from an adequate income or resources; material deprivation and low income (reported in previous chapters); exclusion from the labour market; exclusion from decent housing; exclusion from public and private services; and exclusion from social participation and networks, including personal insecurity and imprisonment.

The labour market

Exclusion from the labour market is a major problem in a society where identity, self esteem and income are based on paid work. It is one of the main causes of deprivation, contributes to ill-health and impacts on social relations. In Northern Ireland at the end of 2002 and the beginning of 2003, 13.6 per cent of all households (excluding pensioner households) had no adult in the household in paid work. In contrast over one third of all households had two or more workers in them. Over one fifth of all households are composed of retired people (Figure 7.1).

Figure 7.1: *Labour market exclusion, type of household*

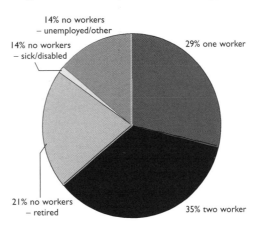

14% no workers
– unemployed/other

14% no workers
– sick/disabled

29% one worker

21% no workers
– retired

35% two worker

Housing

In Northern Ireland two thirds of all housing is owner-occupied. The other third is rented from the Northern Ireland Housing Executive (NIHE), housing associations or a private or commercial landlord. The NIHE reports an ongoing increase in homelessness, with 14,164 households presenting as homeless in 2001/2002, an increase of 10 per cent on the previous year (NIHE, 2003a). These figures suggests that well over one in three households have missed out on a range of advantages which have accrued to owner occupiers over the last decade: a reasonably wide choice of housing, much of it new; increased property values; and access to bank and consumer credit. Those in social housing or those who are homeless have been excluded in a very material sense from the benefits which most of the other two thirds of the population have had from owner occupation. While some people do not own their own home, the survey reveals that some 6.5 per cent of the population own a second home and over 2 per cent of the population own other houses apart from their current residence or a second home or holiday home.

The NIHE recently conducted a large scale house condition survey (NIHE, 2003b). It shows that, while housing unfitness has declined since the last survey in 1996, some 5 per cent of all houses in Northern Ireland are unfit. In addition the survey found that one third of all dwellings in Northern Ireland required urgent attention. In the PSENI survey households reported a range of problems with their houses. Over 10 per cent reported problems with the lack of space, 7.3 per cent with damp walls, floors etc, and 4.6 per cent with rot in the window frames or floor.

Public and private services

Respondents were asked about a range of different public and private services to ascertain their accessibility, desirability and adequacy. If they did not use a service they were asked whether this was because they did not want it or because they could not afford it. It was thus possible to distinguish between 'collective exclusion' where services were unavailable to everyone in a particular area or unsuitable, and 'individual exclusion' where services existed but individuals could not access them due to lack of money. The PSEB survey asked the same set of social exclusion questions and the responses are noted in brackets in Table 7.1 for comparison.

Table 7.1 shows that, like Britain, the main difficulty in relation to services is unavailability rather than not being able to afford the service. In public transport for instance no one was excluded from its use because of lack of

Table 7.1: *Exclusion from public and private services, PSENI (and PSEB)*

	Collective exclusion			Individual exclusion	
	Use – adequate	Use – inadequate	Don't use – unavailable or unsuitable	Don't use – can't afford	Don't use or not relevant
Public services					
Libraries	38 (55)	3 (16)	5 (3)	0 (0)	54 (36)
Public sports facilities	36 (39)	3 (7)	7 (5)	1 (1)	53 (48)
Museums and galleries	25 (29)	1 (4)	14 (13)	1 (1)	59 (52)
Evening classes	13 (17)	1 (2)	9 (5)	2 (3)	75 (73)
Public community/village hall	21 (31)	2 (3)	9 (9)	0 (0)	69 (56)
Hospital with A&E	66 (75)	17 (13)	0 (2)	0 (0)	17 (10)
Doctor	90 (92)	7 (6)	0 (0)	0 (0)	3 (2)
Dentist	86 (83)	2 (5)	0 (1)	0 (0)	11 (11)
Optician	72 (78)	0 (3)	1 (1)	1 (1)	26 (17)
Post Office	93 (93)	3 (4)	0 (0)	0 (0)	3 (2)
Public transport	38 (38)	9 (15)	9 (6)	0	0
Private services					
Places of worship	65 (30)	1 (1)	0 (2)	1 (0)	33 (66)
Pay phone	24 (37)	3 (10)	5 (10)	0 (1)	67 (41)
Petro station	63 (75)	2 (2)	2 (2)	0 (1)	33 (21)
Chemist	96 (93)	1 (3)	1 (1)	0 (0)	3 (3)
Corner shop	80 (73)	2 (7)	9 (8)	0 (0)	10 (12)
Medium to large supermarket	91 (92)	2 (4)	2 (2)	0 (0)	6 (2)
Banks or building societies	80 (87)	4 (7)	3 (1)	2 (0)	12 (4)
Bar	44 (53)	1 (4)	2 (2)	2 (2)	50 (37)
Cinema or theatre	52 (45)	2 (6)	7 (10)	3 (5)	36 (33)

money but a significant proportion, nearly a tenth (9 per cent), were excluded from the service because it was either unavailable or unsuitable (for example only accessible to able bodied people). There were similar results for a corner shop and a community village hall. Access to these kinds of facilities is particularly important for some social groups such the elderly, parents of young children and the disabled, for all of whom social participation and inclusion through paid work is relatively unlikely.

The survey also asked questions about domestic services such as gas, electricity and telephone and whether these services had ever been disconnected from their home or their use restricted. Overall, 5.4 per cent had had these basic domestic services disconnected one or more times.

Exclusion from social participation

At this stage of analysis of the PSENI research, exclusion from social participation is reported in terms of inability to engage in a range of common social activities because of lack of money. Three activities have been included because, although a majority of the public did not think they were necessities, they are useful indicators of social exclusion and its converse social inclusion. The three are: 'going out for an evening meal once a fortnight', 'holiday abroad once a year', and 'going out for

Table 7.1: *Number of common social activities that cannot be afforded*

	%	cumulative %
None	56	56
1	12	68
2	8	76
3-4	11	88
5 or more	12	100

meal in a restaurant once a month'. Just over half (56 per cent) of households could afford to participate in all the social activities listed in the survey (including the three not thought to be necessities). Twelve per cent of households could not participate in one social activity because of lack of money, 8 per cent in two and 12 per cent in five or more.

Personal insecurity

Personal safety and freedom from interpersonal violence is one of the foundation stones of a modern democratic society. People who are killed and injured are denied one of the most basic human rights as are those who fear death or injury at the hands of others. They can, therefore, be seen as excluded from a 'normal' life in a very real and tangible way. Over the last 30 years of conflict in Northern Ireland over 3,600 people have been killed and tens of thousands injured.

The survey asked a series of questions about the conflict. Overall, 50 per cent of respondents said they knew someone who had been killed in the 'troubles', but this figure falls to 30 per cent for those who lost close friends and/or relatives. The relatively high proportions for 'close friend' and 'close relative' in Figure 7.2 suggest that respndents may have interpreted these questions rather loosely. It should also be pointed out that there is overlap between the categories – for instance 11 per cent said they had lost a close friend *and* a close relative.

Figure 7.2 shows that over a quarter of respondents stated that a 'close friend' had been killed and of these 45 per cent had lost two or more close friends. In addition, 14 per cent of respondents had had a 'close relative' killed and of these over 20 per cent had lost two or more relatives. Finally, nearly two fifths knew 'someone else' who had been killed and of these over two thirds knew two or more people who had been killed. Half of the 'someone else' category did not lose a close friend or relative in the 'troubles'.

Figure 7.3 shows the number of people who had experienced some sort of physical injury either to themselves or someone else. In total nearly 8 per cent of all respondents had been injured during the 'troubles' and of these some 50 per cent had been injured on two or more occasions. Just over a quarter had

Figure 7.2: *Knowing someone killed in the 'troubles'*

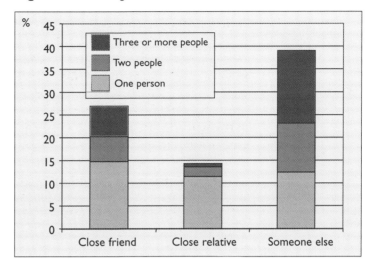

Figure 7.3: *Experience of physical injury*

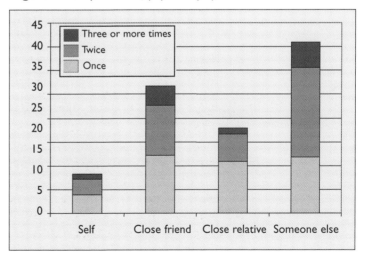

a close friend who had been physically injured and of these 45.8 per cent had been injured on one occasion and over 53 per cent a few or many times. Nearly 18 per cent had a close relative who had been injured and nearly 36 per cent knew someone else personally who had been injured. Of these two groups some 60 per cent and 67 per cent, respectively, had been injured more than once.

Further evidence of widespread exclusion from personal safety in Northern Ireland over the last 30 years is shown in other data. Some 8.6 per cent of HRs had had to move house due to attack, intimidation or harassment and 4.4 per cent had been forced to leave a job for the same reasons.

Imprisonment

A final form of exclusion considered in the survey was imprisonment, defined in terms of whether the household respondent or someone they knew had spent time in prison. Nearly a quarter of all respondents had themselves spent time in prison or knew someone else who had. Where they themselves had been in prison (5 per cent), some two thirds were not now living in poor households.

Conclusion

This chapter has considered some of the main dimensions of social exclusion in Northern Ireland. Further analysis is needed to explore possible relationships within and between dimensions, the cumulative impact of exclusion and the types of households most affected. The main point to emphasise at this stage is that social exclusion is extensive.

Perhaps the most significant finding is that one in every eight households in Northern Ireland (excluding pensioner households) has no one in paid work. This denies these households access to adequate material resources and severely restricts their integration into a range of social and civic activities. It impacts on the future as well as the present children in the household and it has wide-ranging social costs in terms of ill-health, relationship breakdown and other problems. Social exclusion in whatever form has widespread implications which go beyond the individual to neighbourhoods and social order as a whole.

Chapter 8
Conclusions

This book has presented the main findings of the first ever large-scale quantitative study of poverty and social exclusion in Northern Ireland. It has confirmed evidence from administrative social security data and from other research that high levels of poverty and social exclusion exist in Northern Ireland. It has provided a baseline measurement of both poverty and social exclusion which can be updated periodically in the future. It has also provided data across the section 75 dimensions specified in the Northern Ireland Act which may be used as benchmarks against which to assess the extent to which public authorities have carried out their statutory duty to promote equality of opportunity. Finally, it has enabled comparison of poverty rates between Northern Ireland, Britain and the Republic of Ireland.

The study has documented and explained the most fundamental challenge at the heart of poverty research and political debate: how to define and measure the nature and extent of poverty. As discussed in Chapter 3, there are two main types of approaches to the measurement of poverty: those based on income alone and those which combine income with other indicators of deprivation. Both also vary according to the income equivalence scale adopted and judgements about the appropriate cut-off points for 'poverty lines'. The second broad approach, combining income and deprivation, as we have seen, has consisted of two variants: the consistent poverty approach used in the Republic of Ireland and the PSE consensual poverty approach developed in Britain.

All measures of poverty have their

limitations *(handwritten margin note)*

Personal choices *(handwritten margin note)*

limitations. To summarise the limitations of income only measures: income is an indirect measure; they fail to capture the effects of publicly provided goods or services on standards of living; they vary greatly over time; they provide a measure of a person's monetary resources and not the result of their application of those resources; the choice of one particular income measure is so much a matter of judgement it is arbitrary. There is no scientific reason why less than 60 per cent of the mean or 70 per cent of the median should be used. Whichever is chosen reflects the personal choices of administrators or politicians.

Mixed income-deprivation measures recognise and redress these limitations. Where they differ is in the choice of deprivation indicators. In the Republic of Ireland consistent poverty measure, the items of deprivation were selected by experts using statistical techniques. In the consensual poverty measure, the indicators are chosen by a simple majority of the people in the society concerned. Subsequent identification of the poverty threshold – the point which best distinguishes the poor from the non-poor – is based on statistical procedures. Within these procedures, some choices do have to be made by the researchers, for example the equivalisation scale to use and how best to deal with outliers in the income

data. Nonetheless the consensual method provides the most objective, democratic, independent and non-arbitrary measure of poverty devised to date. *185,000 - Poor House (handwritten)*

These first ever statistically reliable findings on poverty in Northern Ireland are staggering. More than one hundred and eighty five thousand households are poor and over half a million people live in poor households. There are marked important and significant differences in poverty rates between different social groups. The disabled are nearly twice as likely to be in poverty as the non-disabled. The youngest group of households are twice as likely to be in poverty compared with the oldest. Women are more likely to be poor than men. The level of poverty is 1.4 times as high in households where the household respondent is Catholic compared with households where the household respondent is Protestant. Many people however will think the most significant finding is that well over a third (37.4 per cent) of all this society's children are being brought up in poverty. The impact on the development and opportunities of these 150,000 children and young people should not be under-estimated. The wider consequences and costs for society as a whole must also be of concern. These children and young people occupy what Byrne (2002) has vividly described as the 'spaces of dispossession', growing up as excluded people in excluded families increasingly characterised by anti-social behaviour, insecurity and threat.

Less than two thirds of all children in Northern Ireland have a lifestyle and living standard regarded by a representative sample of all people as an acceptable basic norm. While the divisions around religion, national identity and political preference dominate all discussions in the media, in local council chambers and in the Assembly, this study has turned the spotlight to other equally important but less visible divisions of class, gender, age and disability.

The challenge for Northern Ireland as a whole and the local politicians, in particular, is how to reduce these deep fractures of inequality. A progressive equality framework including Section 75 of the Northern Ireland Act, New Targeting Social Need and incorporated human rights legislation is now in place. Does the political will and social consensus exist to harness that framework to the eradication of child poverty? Local politicians face an important constraint in that some key policies, namely fiscal and social security matters remain the responsibility of Westminster not a Stormont government. Taking the eradication of child poverty seriously would involve a substantial redistribution of resources and whether those who would lose out would support such a fundamental shift in current economic arrangements must be at the heart of future political debate.

We have a moral responsibility to all the children.

Bibliography

Balanda, K.P. and Wilde, J. (2001) *Inequalities in Mortality, 1989-1998, A Report on All-Ireland Mortality Data*, IPA.

Bradshaw, J. (1993) *Budget Standards for the United Kingdom*, Avebury: Aldershot.

Byrne, D. (2001) *Social Exclusion,* Buckingham: Open University Press.

Civic Forum (2002) *A Regional Strategy for Social Inclusion: A Civic Forum Discussion Paper*, Prepared for the Civic Forum Anti-Poverty Project Group, Civic Forum, April 2002.

Department for Work and Pensions (2001) *Opportunity for all — Making Progress Third Annual Report 2001*. Cm. 5260. London: HMSO.

Department for Work and Pensions (2003a) *Households Below Average Income 2001/02.*

Department for Work and Pensions (2003b) *Measuring Child Poverty.*

Dignan, T. and McLaughlin, E. (2002) *New TSN Research: Poverty in Northern Ireland,* Belfast: Office of the First Minister and Deputy First Minister.

Dignan, T. (2003) *Low Income Households in Northern Ireland 1990 - 2000,* Belfast: Office of the First Minister and Deputy First Minister.

Eurostat (2003) *Poverty and social exclusion in the EU after Laeken* – parts 1 and 2, 8/2003 and 9/2003, Luxembourg.

Giddens, A. (1998) *The Third Way: The Renewal of Social Democracy*, Cambridge: Polity Press.

Gordon D., Adelman, L., Ashworth, K., Bradshaw, J., Levitas, R., Middleton, S. Pantazis, C., Patsios, D., Payne, S., Townsend, P. and Williams, J. (2000a) *Poverty and Social Exclusion in Britain*, York: Joseph Rowntree Foundation.

Gordon, D., Pantazis C. and Townsend, P. (2000b) 'Absolute and overall poverty: a European history and proposal for measurement', chapter 5 in D. Gordon and P. Townsend (eds.) *Breadline Europe: The measurement of poverty*. Bristol: Policy Press, pp. 79-105.

Government of Ireland (1997) *Sharing in Progress: National Anti-Poverty Strategy*. Dublin: The Stationery Office.

Howarth, C., Kenway, P., Palmer, G. and Miorelli, R. (1999) *Monitoring Poverty and Social Exclusion 1999*. York: Joseph Rowntree Foundation.

Kaplan, G. A., Pamuk, E. R., Lynch, J. W., Cohen, R. D. and Balfour, J. L. (1996) 'Inequality in Income and Mortality in the United States: Analysis of Mortality and Potential Pathways', *British Medical Journal,* Vol. 312, April 20, pp. 999–1003.

Kennedy, P., Kawachi, J. and Prothrow-Stith, D. (1996) 'Income distribution and mortality: cross sectional ecological study of the Robin Hood Index in the United States', *British Medical Journal*, Vol. 312, pp. 1004-1007.

Levitas, R. (1998) *The Inclusive Society? Social Exclusion and New Labour*. London: Macmillan.

Mack, J. and Lansley, S. (1985) *Poor Britain*, London: Allen and Unwin.

McAuley, C., Hillyard, P., McLaughlin, E., Tomlinson, M., Kelly, G. and Patsios, D. (2003) Working Paper No. 1, *The Necessities of Life in Northern Ireland*, Belfast: School of Sociology and Social Policy, Queen's University Belfast.

McClelland, A. and Gribbin, V. (2002) *Evaluation of New TSN: Gini Coefficient Analyses*, Office of the First Minister and Deputy First Minister, Equality Directorate Research Branch.

McGregor, P. and McKee, P. (1995) 'A Widening Gap?' in *Social Exclusion*, Democratic Dialogue, Report No. 2. Belfast: Democratic Dialogue.

Middleton, S. *et al*, (1997) *Family Fortunes: pressures on parents and children in the 1990s*, London: Child Poverty Action Group.

Noble, M., Smith, G., Wright, G., Dibben, C. and Lloyd, M. (2001) *The Northern Ireland Multiple Deprivation Measure 2001*. Belfast: Northern Ireland Statistics and Research Agency.

Nolan, B., Gannon, B., Layte, R., Watson, D., Whelan, C. and Williams, J. (2002) *Monitoring Poverty Trends in Ireland: Results from the 2000 Living in Ireland Survey*. Dublin: Economic and Social Research Institute.

Northern Ireland Executive (2001) *Programme for Government*, Belfast.

Northern Ireland Housing Executive (2003a) *Northern Ireland Housing Executive Housing Agenda 02/03*, Belfast: NIHE.

Northern Ireland Housing Executive (2003b) *Northern Ireland House Condition Survey, 2001*, Belfast: NIHE.

Palmer, G., Rahman, M. and Kenway, P. (2002) *Monitoring poverty and social exclusion 2002*, York: Joseph Rowntree Foundation.

Quirk, P. & McLaughlin, E. (1996) 'Targeting Social Need', in E. McLaughlin and P. Quirk (eds.) *Policy Aspects of Employment Equality in Northern Ireland, Employment Equality in Northern Ireland Vol II*. Belfast: Standing Advisory Commission on Human Rights.

Rahman, M., Palmer, G., Kenway, P. and Howarth, C. (2000) *Monitoring Poverty and Social Exclusion 2000*, York: Joseph Rowntree Foundation.

Rahman, M., Palmer, G. and Kenway, P. (2001) *Monitoring poverty and social exclusion 2001,* York: Joseph Rowntree Foundation.

Scottish Executive (2002) *Annex to the Social Justice Annual Report 2002*. Edinburgh: Scottish Executive.

Shaw, M., Dorling, D., Gordon, D. & Smith, G.D. (1999) *The Widening Gap: Health Inequalities and Policy in Britain*, Bristol: The Policy Press.

Tomlinson, M. (2000) 'Targeting Social Need, Social Exclusion and the Use of Social Security Statistics' in N. Yeates and E. McLaughlin (eds.) *Measuring Social Exclusion and Poverty*, pp. 90-128. Belfast: Department for Social Development.

Tomlinson, M. (2001) 'Unemployment and Inactivity': Comparing Ireland, North and South', in N. Yeates and G. P. Kelly, *Poverty and Social Security: Comparing Ireland North and South*. Belfast: Department for Social Development.

Tomlinson, M. and Kelly, G. P. (2003) 'What's the Use of the Noble Index? Theories, Methods and Applications', in *Edging Poverty Out: Anti-Poverty Strategies in Ireland, North and South*. Belfast: Department for Social Development.

Townsend, P. (1979) *Poverty in the United Kingdom*, Harmondsworth: Penguin.

United Nations (1995) *Report of the World Summit for Social Development* (Copenhagen 6-12 March). New York: United Nations.

Appendix
Technical Report

This technical report was supplied by the Central Survey Unit, Northern Ireland Statistical and Research Agency.

1. The Sample

A sample of 3,490 addresses was drawn from the Valuation and Lands Agency (VLA) list of addresses. The VLA list is the most up to date listing of private households. People living in institutions (though not private households in such institutions) are excluded.

The complete VLA list of private addresses is stratified into three regions – Belfast, East of Northern Ireland and West of Northern Ireland. The number of addresses drawn from each region is in proportion to the number of addresses in the region. The sample is therefore equivalent to a simple random sample of all private addresses in Northern Ireland.

The Valuation and Lands Agency provides a good sampling frame of addresses, but contains no information about the number of households living at an address. Further selection stages are therefore required to decide which household to interview.

Interviewers are instructed to call at each address issued in their assignments. If an interviewer comes across an address, which contains more than one household, then a decision must be made as to which household to select to take part in the interview. The interviewer then numbers each individual household and uses Table 1.1 to determine which one of the households to interview:

Table 1.1: *Household Selection Table*

Number of Households	2	3	4	5	6	7
Household Selected	1	3	2	2	6	4

2. Information collected

The questionnaire was split into a core section and two optional sections, one of which was asked of each of the respondents. The list below shows how the modules were asked.

CORE
  Household Section
  Household questions

  Individual Section
  Demography
  Necessities and economising
  Opinions on standard of living
  Intra-household living standards
  Views on poverty level
  Health and disability
  [Optional modules A OR B] See below
  Economic activity
  Income
  Assets and debt
  Self completion section

OPTIONAL
Module A	*Module B*
Area Characteristics	Activism
Community Support	Local Services
	Mobility
	The Troubles

Modules A and B were randomly assigned to individuals in the household.

Table 3.1: *Response Rate*

	Number	Relative Frequency	Response Rate (Eligible Sample)
Issued addresses	3490		
Eligible sample	3110	89%	100%
Interview achieved all adults	1425	57%	64%
Interview Achieved at least 1 adult	551		
Household interview only	15		
Refusal	750	21%	24%
Non-contact	369	11%	12%
Non-eligible	380	11%	

3. The Fieldwork

Addresses were issued to a panel of 115 interviewers. The fieldwork period was 14 October 2002 to the 31st January 2003.

4. Representativeness of the Sample

In any survey there is a possibility of non-response bias. Non-response bias arises if the characteristics of non-respondents differ from those of respondents in such a way that they are reflected in the responses given in the survey. Accurate estimates of non-response bias can be obtained by comparing characteristics of the achieved sample with the distribution of the same characteristics in the population at the time of sampling. Such comparisons are usually made to the current Census of Population data.

To assess how accurately the survey sample reflects the population of Northern Ireland the sample has been compared with characteristics of the Northern Ireland population from the 2001 Census of Population (Table 4.1). The sample has also been compared to the achieved sample of the Continuous Household Survey (CHS).

Comparison was also made using the Noble Multiple Deprivation Index. The tables below (Table 4.2 and 4.3) show the figures for the random sample drawn at the beginning of the questionnaire and the same figures for the achieved addresses.

Table 4.1

	2001 Census	CHS 2001/02 (all members of household 16+)	Poverty study (all members of household 16+)
Age			
<25	16	15	16
25-44	38	38	39
45-64	28	29	29
65 and over	17	18	15
Gender			
Male	48	47	47
Female	52	53	53
Base=100%	1,292,169	5,545	3,853

Table 4.2: *Multiple Deprivation Measure for drawn sample*

	Frequency	Percent	Valid Percent
0 - 4.9	344	9.9	10.0
5.0 - 9.9	629	18.0	18.3
10.0 - 14.9	596	17.1	17.4
25.0 - 19.9	357	10.2	10.4
20.0 - 29.9	648	18.6	18.9
30.0 - 39.9	385	11.0	11.2
40.0 - 49.9	195	5.6	5.7
50.0 - 59.9	113	3.2	3.3
60.0 - 69.9	102	2.9	3.0
70.0 - 79.9	60	1.7	1.7
Total	3429	98.3	100.0
Postcode not matched	61	1.7	
Total	3490	100.0	

Table 4.3: *Multiple Deprivation Measure for achieved sample*

	Frequency	Percent	Valid Percent
0 - 4.9	187	9.4	9.5
5.0 - 9.9	359	18.0	18.3
10.0 - 14.9	346	17.4	17.7
25.0 - 19.9	210	10.5	10.7
20.0 - 29.9	373	18.7	19.0
30.0 - 39.9	208	10.4	10.6
40.0 - 49.9	103	5.2	5.3
50.0 - 59.9	65	3.3	3.3
60.0 - 69.9	67	3.4	3.4
70.0 - 79.9	42	2.1	2.1
Total	1960	98.4	100.0
Postcode not matched	31	1.6	
Total	1991	100.0	

The figures for the Poverty Study compare favourably with those from the CHS 2001/02 with regards to employment status as shown in Table 4.4.

Table 4.4

	CHS 2001/02 (all members of household interviewed 16+)	Poverty Study
Worked last week	49	53
Away from work last week	2	2
Waiting to take up work	0	0
Looking for work	3	2
Not looking for work – sick	1	1
Economically inactive	41	41
Government training scheme		0
Base = 100%	5,545	3,104

Table 4.5 shows a comparison of the employment groupings with those collected in the 2001 Census.

Table 4.5

All persons aged 16 -74 in employment	Census 2001	Poverty Study
Managers and senior officials	11	9
Professional occupations	11	10
Associate professional and technical occupations	13	11
Administrative occupations	15	14
Skilled trade occupations	16	13
Personal services occupations	7	9
Sales and customer services occupations	7	8
Process plant and machine operatives	10	11
Elementary occupations	12	15
Base = 100%	686,644	2,674

In terms of the industrial sector in which the respondents worked (Table 4.6), the greatest proportion of the respondents worked in the manufacturing sector (14%). Again the figures for CHS 2001/02 are included for comparison.

Table 4.6

	CHS 2001/02 (all members of household interviewed 16+)	Poverty Study
Agriculture	3	3
Fishing	0	0
Mineral and ore extraction	0	0
Manufacturing	13	14
Electrical and gas	1	0
Construction	9	6
Wholesale	12	13
Hotels and restaurants	4	4
Transportation & communication	4	5
Financial intermediaries	2	2
Real estate	4	4
Public administration	9	9
Education	11	10
Health	13	12
Other community services	3	8
Private household	0	0
Insufficient/Dont know/Refusal	11	8
Base = 100%	5,545	3,104

Table 4.7

	CHS 2001/02 (all members of household interviewed 16+)	Poverty Study
Professional	3	4
Employer, manager	7	9
Intermediate non manual	15	18
Junior non manual	16	18
Skilled manual	20	18
Semi-skilled manual	19	20
Unskilled manual	6	7
No SEG, ref, etc., armed forces	14	8
Base = 100%	5,545	3,104

5. Sampling Error

No sample is likely to reflect precisely the characteristics of the population it is drawn from because of both sampling and non-sampling errors. An estimate of the amount of error due to the sampling process can be calculated. For a simple random sample design, in which every member of the sampled population has an equal and independent chance of inclusion in the sample, the sampling error of any percentage, p, can be calculated by the formula:

$$\text{s.e. (p)} = \sqrt{p*(100 - p)/n}$$

where n is the number of respondents on which the percentage is based. The sample for the NI Omnibus Survey is drawn as a random sample, and thus this formula can be used to calculate the sampling error of any percentage estimate from the survey.

A confidence interval for the population percentage can be calculated by the formula

95 per cent confidence interval = p+/- 1.96 * s.e. (p)

If 100 similar, independent samples were chosen from the same population, 95 of them would be expected to yield an estimate for the percentage, p, within this confidence interval.

The absence of design effects in the survey, and therefore of the need to calculate complex standard errors, means that standard statistical tests of significance (which assume random sampling) can be applied directly to the data.

Table 5.1 provides examples of the sampling errors and confidence intervals for typical percentage estimates from the Poverty study, based on the sample size for the complete fieldwork period. These can be used as a rough guide when interpreting results from the survey.

Table 5.1

	(%) (P)	Standard Error of (P) (%)	95% Confidence Interval +/-
Gender n=3104			
Male	47	0.9	1.8
Female	53	0.9	1.8
Managing money n=1888 We mostly keep our money separate	21	0.9	1.8
Your partner and yourself work out how to pay it together	64	1.1	2.2
Meals on wheels n=553 Don't use meals on wheels	98	0.6	1.2